CONTENTS

BASICS

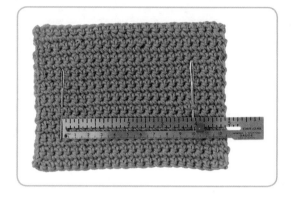

HOOKS AND GAUGE

Hooks come in several different sizes and shapes, depending on their intended uses. But they all have the same parts, labeled in the photo below.

Gauge is a measure of the size of each stitch. Patterns tell the size of the designer's stitches, and if a finished project is to be the stated size, your stitches must be the same size. Gauge is stated as the number of stitches and rows equal to a number of inches, usually 4" (10 cm). To measure gauge, crochet a piece slightly larger than 4" (10 cm). Place two pins in the work 4" (10 cm) apart. Count the stitches between the pins. If you have more stitches than the designated number, you are stitching tighter than average; try a new swatch with a larger hook. If you have fewer stitches than designated, you are stitching looser than average; try a smaller hook.

Yarn labels tell you the "weight" of the yarn, often using a numbering system, and they tell you the suggested hook size and gauge for the yarn. When following pattern projects where gauge is critical, select yarn with the same gauge designated by the project designer. Then test your gauge and adjust hook size until you are crocheting at the correct gauge before starting the project.

The hook included with this kit is US size H/8 (5 mm), the size recommended for the medium-weight acrylic yarn that is included for practice and for making a scarf.

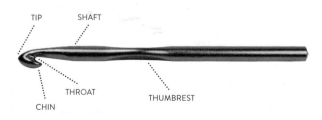

TIP   SHAFT

THROAT   THUMBREST

CHIN

ABOUT YARN

Yarn suitable for crocheting comes in various styles.

Smooth or plain textured yarns are the easiest to crochet with, and allow special textures in the actual stitches to show to best advantage.

Loft is the ability of a yarn to be squeezed smaller (feel "squishy"), and to naturally expand to fill space. Loft is created by air space between the fibers in the yarn.

Twist—the tightness and direction that the fibers are spun together to create the yarn.

Ply—smaller strands of spun fiber that are twisted together to create yarn. A "single" is not plied; its fibers are spun in only one direction. When singles are twisted together, they form a yarn less likely to kink and knot in use. "Worsted" yarn is often made of 4 plies; DK or "Sport" of 3.

Halo—any visible fibers sticking out from the main, twisted core of the yarn. These create a fuzzy texture in the yarn, and in fabric made from the yarn.

Thick and thin—just as it sounds. Some yarns are intentionally varying in their diameter.

Slubs are intentional blobs of unspun or knotted fiber, included in the yarn to add textural interest.

Bouclé refers to loops in yarn, created by twisting two plies together at different rates of speed. The loops can be large or small, and create a haloed effect, as the loops spread out from the yarn's core.

Bloom—refers to a yarn's ability to expand or develop a halo after the fabric is made. Yarns that bloom may start out with a smooth or plain texture, but later develop a fuzzy surface.

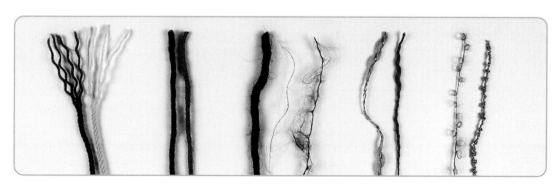

From left to right: smooth or plain with several plies, smooth single, yarns with halo, plied thick and thin with slubs, bouclé yarn

ABBREVIATIONS

Here is the list of the most common abbreviations used for crochet.

approx.	approximately	**p**	picot
beg	begin/beginning	**patt**	pattern
bet	between	**pc**	popcorn
BL	back loop(s)	**pm**	place marker
bo	bobble	**prev**	previous
BP	back post	**rem**	remain/remaining
CC	contrasting color	**rep**	repeat(s)
ch	chain	**rnd(s)**	round(s)
ch-	refers to chain or space previously made, e.g., ch-1 space	**RS**	right side(s)
		sc	single crochet
ch lp	chain loop	**sc2tog**	single crochet 2 stitches together
ch-sp	chain space	**sk**	skip
CL	cluster(s)	**Sl st**	slip stitch
cm	centimeter(s)	**sp(s)**	space(s)
cont	continue	**st(s)**	stitch(es)
dc	double crochet	**tbl**	through back loop(s)
dc2tog	double crochet 2 stitches together	**tch**	turning chain
dec	decrease/decreases/decreasing	**tfl**	through front loop(s)
FL	front loop(s)	**tog**	together
foll	follow/follows/following	**tr**	triple crochet
FP	front post	**WS**	wrong side(s)
g	gram(s)	**yd**	yard(s)
hdc	half double crochet	**yo**	yarn over
inc	increase/increases/increasing	**[ ]**	Work instructions within brackets as many times as directed.
lp(s)	loop(s)		
m	meter(s)	*****	Repeat instructions following the single asterisk as directed.
MC	main color		
mm	millimeter(s)	*** ***	Repeat instructions between asterisks as many times as directed or repeat from a given set of instructions.
oz	ounce(s)		

READING SYMBOLS

Crochet designers use a set of international stitch symbols. When arranged in a chart, they resemble the finished crochet design. While most crochet projects are presented in written form, many are also accompanied by a chart, and you can follow either or both while crocheting your project. Below is a chart of some of the more common stitch symbols.

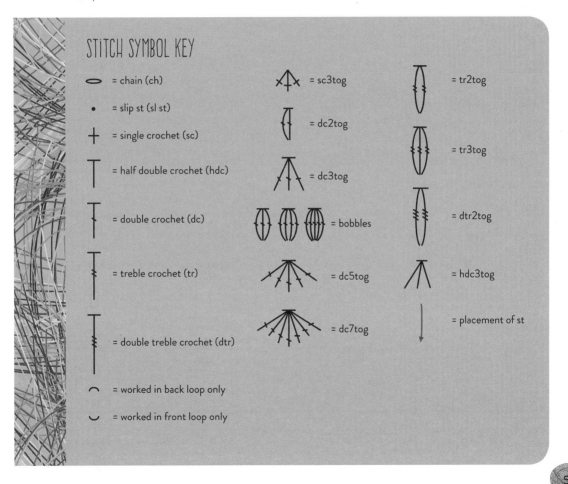

STITCH SYMBOL KEY

- ⬭ = chain (ch)
- • = slip st (sl st)
- ✝ = single crochet (sc)
- T = half double crochet (hdc)
- ↨ = double crochet (dc)
- ↨ = treble crochet (tr)
- ↨ = double treble crochet (dtr)
- ⌒ = worked in back loop only
- ⌣ = worked in front loop only

- ✕⋀✕ = sc3tog
- ⨏ = dc2tog
- ⋀ = dc3tog
- ◍◍◍ = bobbles
- ⋀ = dc5tog
- ⋀ = dc7tog

- ⨑ = tr2tog
- ◍ = tr3tog
- ⨑ = dtr2tog
- ⋀ = hdc3tog
- ↓ = placement of st

HOW TO HOLD THE HOOK

There is no one "right way" to hold the crochet hook, but some are more effective, efficient, and healthier for the hand and wrist than others. The three most common hook holds are the Pencil Hold, the Knife Hold, and the Chopstick Hold.

The **Pencil Hold** looks graceful but it requires much more movement of the wrist in every stitch, which can lead to repetitive stress injuries, such as carpal tunnel syndrome.

The **Chopstick Hold** is similar, in that it requires constant bend in the wrist, and also places the least coordinated fingers in position to control loops of yarn on the hook. However, many crocheters continue to find one of these to be their preferred hold, and can be successful by taking extra breaks to rest the wrist, and/or wearing a supportive fingerless glove.

The **Knife Hold** provides increased control of loops on the hook and increased comfort for the hand and wrist. This overhand method has gained popularity as the crafting population has grown more concerned with fun and health than with elegance. Try the different holds to find the best style for your hands.

Most people will hold the hook in the right hand, and the yarn in the left hand. Because crochet uses both hands, even left-handed crocheters are not disadvantaged, and often find it a distinct advantage to hold and move the yarn, instead of the hook, with their dominant hand. However, some "lefties" do prefer to hold the hook in the left hand, and reverse for themselves all directional instructions. Whether to move the yarn more, or the hook more, is a personal decision, but in either case, there is an initial period of feeling awkward, regardless of hand preference!

Pencil Hold—hook over top of hand, between thumb and first finger

Chopstick Hold—hook over top of hand, between fingers

Knife or Overhand Hold—hand over top of hook, wrist in neutral position

HOW TO HOLD THE YARN

There is also no one "right" way to hold the yarn, and each crocheter goes through a process of experimentation to find a satisfactory balance between firm control and necessary flow as the yarn is used in each stitch. The photos here show three common, effective methods. Notice that in each, the index finger is extended, ready to move the yarn where needed, and that other fingers regulate the tension or flow of the yarn as it is used.

Don't be afraid to experiment, and don't expect to settle a yarn hold in the first few projects! It takes time and repetition for fingers and yarn to become accustomed to working together.

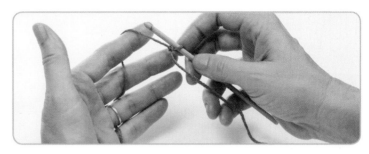

"Woven" yarn hold: Yarn from the working ball simply passes over and under alternate fingers. Tension is increased by squeezing fingers together when needed.

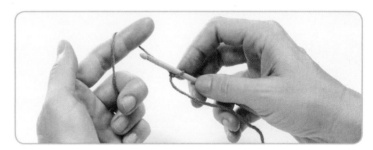

Simple "fist" hold: Yarn from the working ball is held in the fist. Tension is increased by closing the fist.

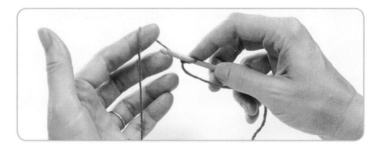

Looped tension hold: Yarn passes between pinkie and ring fingers, around pinkie and across palm, then around index finger. Tension is increased by curling the pinkie finger and holding it against ring finger.

HOW TO CROCHET

This kit contains two colors of yarn, 120 yd (110 m) of each. The scarf project on page 28 requires at least 80 yd (74 m) of each color. Use the extra yarn for practice.

Yarn loop with tail behind.

THE SLIP KNOT

All crochet begins with a slip knot. Start by making a loop, about 8" (20.5 cm) from the end of the yarn, with the yarn tail away from you, behind the circle that's been formed. Push the tail through to form a loop; tighten the loop by pulling the yarn attached to the main ball.

Place the slip knot on the hook, with the working yarn (the end connected to the ball) away from you.

When a slip knot is formed correctly, pulling on the tail will tighten the loop, and pulling on the working yarn will tighten the knot. Pull the tail to snug the loop to the shaft of the hook. It needs to be close enough that "daylight" doesn't show through, but loose enough to move easily up and down the shaft of the hook. Use the index finger to hold that loop in place and prevent it from spinning around the hook. Everything is now in place to make the first crochet stitch!

Pushing tail through to form loop.

THE CHAIN STITCH

Many crochet projects begin with a chain.

1 With the chin of the hook facing you, and the right index finger holding the loop on the hook, the left hand brings the yarn over the top of the hook, from the back, and down across the throat of the hook. The left thumb and second finger pull down on the slip knot to open up a small space at the bottom of the loop on the hook, while the left index finger moves the working yarn.

2 The right hand turns the hook downward, catch-ing the wrapped yarn with the hook, and pulls it through the loop already on the hook. The finger holding the loop on the hook lets go at this point, and will take its place to control the new loop, now on the hook. Do Not pull or tighten the stitch once com-pleted. The chain now being formed serves as a base for the next row of stitches, and must be made loosely.

To count chains, lay the work flat, so that the side with a flat braided or sideways Vs appearance is facing up. Each V is one stitch. Don't count the loop currently on the hook. Start counting with the last V in line before the tight knot at the end and stop at the V immediately below the hook.

Correct direction for yarn over—hook is under yarn as yarn comes over the hook from the back, and down across the hook at the front.

Hook pulling yarn through loop.

Completed first chain stitch.

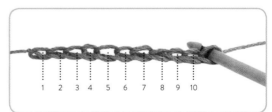

SINGLE CROCHET IN ROWS

Start by making a loose chain of 11 stitches. Single crochet rows always start with one unused chain. This provides space for maneuvering the hook as the row begins, creates an even edge to the fabric being created, and is called the "turning chain." So to begin, locate the second chain from the hook by counting the sideways Vs on the front of the chain. This is the first space in which to work a single crochet stitch. Each chain consists of 3 strands: the lower or front arm of the V is called the Front Loop; the upper or back arm of the V is the Back Loop, and the central strand, best seen from the back of the chain, is usually called the Bottom Bump or Back Bar. Successful fabric can be created by inserting the hook at any of these points in the chain!

Insertion Options

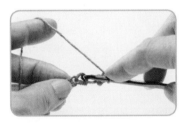

Insertion under Back Loop only: *quick and easy but stretches each stitch and edge will appear unfinished*

Insertion under Front Loop only: *quick and easy but stretches each stitch and edge will appear unfinished*

Insertion under Front and Back Loops: *will not stretch out the stitch, will probably require an edging*

Insertion under Back Loop and Bottom Bump: *will not stretch out the stitch, will probably require an edging*

Insertion under Bottom Bump only: *a little trickier, but creates a completely finished edge, identical to the one that will exist at the other end of the work*

Row 1

1 Insert the hook into the second stitch from the hook, by poking the tip in, from front to back, moving the tip of the hook away from you.

2 Catch the working yarn with the chin of the hook, and pull that new loop toward you through the work, to the front. This step is commonly abbreviated as "yo and draw up a loop." There are now two loops on the hook.

3 Yarn over, and pull the new loop through both of the loops on the hook. This step is abbreviated as "yo and pull through 2." One single crochet stitch is now complete.

4 Locate the next chain, immediately to the left of the stitch just completed. Repeat steps 1 to 3 to form the next single crochet stitch.

5 Continue until each chain has one single crochet stitch in it. There should be 10 single crochets, and they are counted, same as chains, by looking at the sideways Vs along the top edge.

Yarn over at back of work.

Loop drawn up, 2 loops on hook.

Hook pulling yo through 2 loops.

Completed single crochet stitch, arrow shows location of next chain stitch in line.

Completed first row of 10 single crochet (sc) stitches.

Turning the Work

Before beginning Row 2, where single crochets will be worked in the tops of the stitches of Row 1, you must do two things: turn the work so that the unworked tops of Row 1 stretch out to the left, and chain one (the "turning chain"). Many beginners also find it useful to place a stitch marker (paperclip, earring hook, bobby pin, sewing eye) in the top of the first stitch worked in each row.

Look at the row just completed and place a marker in the first stitch you made. The marker can be slipped onto the front or the back loop of the top of the stitch, at the opposite (beginning) end of the row from where the hook is now situated. Also mark the last stitch, the one most recently completed. The first stitch of the following row will be made in this marked stitch, then work in every stitch including the marked stitch at the other end of the row.

Marking helps to make sure every stitch in every row is worked. It doesn't matter which of these (the marking, the ch1, or the turning) is done first, and patterns will specify one way or another at the convenience of the designer. Turn the work as if you were turning the page of a book, with the tops of Row 1's stitches still at the top of the work. Chain 1 (yo and pull through 1 loop), and Row 2 will begin.

Row 2—Working sc into sc

As before, the loop on the hook will not count. The loop immediately below the hook is the turning chain. Locate the first actual stitch of the row, immediately below or to the left of the turning chain. Insert the hook under both the front and back loops. It is possible to work under only one of the loops, but that's a different stitch and creates a different texture to the fabric. The standard way to work all basic crochet stitches is to insert under both loops of the top V. When a pattern intends that only one loop is used, that will be clearly stated.

Complete one sc stitch in each stitch across the row. The three steps of each stitch are the same as for the first row, except that most people find it easier to work into sc stitches than into chains!

Practice single crochet in rows for several more rows.

Ready to start Row 2, marker is first stitch made in Row 1.

Correct hook insertion into a sc.

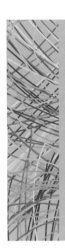

CROCHET LANGUAGE

In a standard pattern, directions for the two rows just completed, will read like this: (Detailed explanations follow each direction, in parenthetic italics)

Foundation—ch 11. (Chain 11)

Row 1: Sc in 2nd ch from hook and in each ch across. Turn. (Make 1 single crochet stitch in the second chain from the hook, and one single crochet in each chain stitch across the row. Turn the work as turning the page in a book)

Row 2: Ch 1, sc in each st across. Turn. (Make 1 chain for the turning chain, make 1 single crochet stitch in the top of each stitch across the row, turn the work).

Finishing

After crocheting a piece of fabric, the instructions will tell you to "fasten off." Cut the working yarn about 8" (20.5 cm) away from the work. Use the hook to pull this tail of yarn right through the last stitch made. The last stitch is now locked and will not unravel. This is the way all crochet ends.

Weave in tails. Thread the tail onto a yarn needle and run it through the inside of a row in one direction, then vertically through two or three rows, then opposite to the first direction in another row.

It's normal for small swatches of single crochet to curl diagonally, from the lower right corner and the upper left corner. This is due to the shape of the stitch. Because curling is more pronounced if the work is a little tight, one way to minimize curling is to work loosely. Most projects will also call for an edging to be worked around the outside of single crocheted pieces, or for seams. Either of these finishing steps usually eliminates the curling. Blocking finished work is another way to flatten it, and project directions usually specify the method for blocking.

Normal curling of edges.

THE DOUBLE CROCHET STITCH

Double crochet is a taller stitch, so every row or round worked increases the height of the fabric piece twice as fast as a row of single crochet does. Double crochet fabric is less solid, less thick, and less stiff; it drapes better and so is ideal for garments and blankets.

Row 1

Start by making a swatch of sc in three or four rows so there is some fabric to hold on to. Although single crochet rows always begin with 1 chain stitch (the "turning chain"), the double crochet stitch needs a taller turning chain because it's a taller stitch. Therefore, to begin the first row of double crochet, chain 3. This is the standard turning chain for double crochet. Because the turning chain is so tall, it will

actually stand in the place of the first stitch of the row. Look at your swatch and locate the first stitch in the row. Place a marker in that stitch, and place a marker in the last of the three chains just made (chain immediately below the loop on the hook).

Turn the work, to begin the row of dc. The marked first stitch of the row will be skipped, and the first actual dc stitch of the row will be made in the stitch immediately to its left.

1 The first difference between a sc and a dc stitch is in how they are begun. The sc stitch began with insertion of the hook into the designated stitch. The dc stitch, however, begins with a yarn over (yo). This is done in the same direction as all yarn overs, back to front, right to left, with the yarn coming over the top of the hook and down in front of it.

Now insert the hook in the second stitch of the row (left of the marker), yo at the back of the work (A) and draw up a loop. There are now three loops on the hook (B).

2 Yarn over and pull that new loop through the first two loops on the hook. This step is designated "yo and pull through 2."

3 There are still two loops on the hook. Yo again, and pull the loop through the two remaining on the hook. A double crochet stitch is completed.

4 To make the second stitch, repeat steps 1–3, inserting the hook in the next stitch in the row.

Yo, insert hook, and draw up a loop.

Yo and pull through 2.

Yo and pull through 2.

5 Continue across the row, till one dc stitch stands in each sc stitch of the previous row. Now move the marker from the skipped stitch at the beginning of the row, and place it in the last stitch of the row, the last stitch made. This will be the skipped stitch at the beginning of the next row. Chain 3, mark the 3rd chain made, and turn the work.

Working Rows of Double Crochet

The second and all following rows begin in the same way as the first: with a ch-3 to turn, skipped first stitch, and then 1 dc in each stitch of the row. As soon as the first stitch of Row 2 is made, remove the marker from the skipped stitch, to use again in a few moments. When the second row is nearly complete, the last stitch of the row will be made into the marked 3rd chain of the previous row's turning chain. In this way, the number of stitches stays the same from row to row and each turning chain "becomes" a dc stitch.

As usual, there are several ways to insert into the chain, but the best appearance of the stitch will be achieved by inserting the hook beneath the front loop and bottom bump. Since the back of that row is facing, these are the top two strands facing you as you look at the turning chain.

Markers show top of turning chain and location of last stitch of Row 2.

Hook inserted beneath front loop and bottom bump of chain.

Completed 2nd row.

THE HALF-DOUBLE CROCHET

Half-doubles create a thicker, more cushiony fabric than the other crochet stitches, and are great for soft sweaters, afghans, or slippers.

Start with a chain of 16.

Row 1: Yarn over, insert hook in 3rd ch from hook, and draw up a loop. So far this is just like starting a double crochet stitch. There are 3 loops on the hook. (A)

Yarn over and pull through all three loops. (1 hdc made) (B)

Work across the row, making one hdc in each chain. Turn the work and ch 2.

Whether that turning chain counts as the first stitch of the row or not is a matter of personal preference. If it is counted as a stitch, that turning chain is noticeably thinner than all the other stitches in the row. On the other hand, if the ch-2 is not counted as a stitch, the edges of the work will have a wavy appearance because of the

At end of the first row, there are 14 hdc stitches and a turning chain of 2 sts.

ch-2 loops at the ends of the rows. This swatch shows some of the options for turning when working in half-double crochet.

Bottom three rows: ch 2 not counted as a stitch, side edge loops evident.

Rows 4–6: Ch 2 counted, holes appear because end stitch is thinner than others.

Rows 7–9: (Sl st, ch 2) counted as a stitch, no holes, but the end stitch is still "thin."

Rows 10–12: Ch 1, draw loop up a little not counted as a stitch, first hdc made in first stitch, no holes, straight edge to fabric, uniform stitches all the way across.

Rows 13–15: (Ch 1, sc, ch 1) counted as a stitch.

THE TRIPLE (OR TREBLE) CROCHET

The treble crochet (tr) stitch is very similar to the double crochet (dc), except that it starts with an extra yarn over, and is completed with an extra "yo and pull through 2 loops," doing that step 3 times instead of the 2 times for dc. The standard turning chain to start a row of trebles is 4 chain.

1 Yarn over twice and insert the hook into the second stitch of the row. Yarn over and draw a loop through the work. There are now four loops on the hook.

2 Yarn over and pull through two loops. Now there are three loops on the hook (A).

Repeat the (yo and pull through 2) two more times, reducing the number of loops on the hook by one, each time (B). After the third repeat, there will be one loop on the hook again, and the first treble stitch is complete (C).

3 Repeat steps 1 and 2, working in each stitch across the row. Chain 4 to start the next row.

4 Work several more rows, until the stitch is familiar and comfortable.

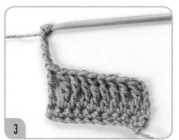

Completed first row of treble stitches, with turning chain to start second row.

Working into the top of the turning chain, to complete Row 2.

17

STITCH COMBINATIONS

GRANNY SQUARES

The classic granny square motif consists of groups of double crochet stitches (usually 3 or 4 stitches per group) separated by chain spaces. Each round is worked in the chain spaces of the previous round, and the corners are formed by working two groups of stitches and their separating space in one corner space.

One Color Granny

Start with ch 4, and slip stitch to join in a ring, thus: insert the hook under 2 strands of the 4th ch from the hook. Yarn over and pull that loop through the chain and through the loop on the hook, at the same time. Joining slip stitch (sl st) made.

Rnd 1: Ch 3 (counts as first dc), work 2 dc in ring, then make a corner increase by working ch 2, (3 dc in ring, ch 2) 3 times, join last ch with a sl st in top of beginning ch 3. At the end of the rnd, there are 4 groups of 3 dc, separated by ch-2 spaces.

Rnd 2: Ch 4 (counts as dc and ch-1), place marker in 3rd ch of the ch-4, skip next group of dc, (3 dc, ch 2, 3 dc) in next ch-2 space. This sequence in parentheses will be repeated at every corner throughout the granny square, no matter how many rounds are made.

*Ch 1, skip next 3-dc group, work corner increase (that is, 3 dc, ch 2, 3 dc) in next ch-2 space; repeat from * one time, ch 1, skip next 3-dc group, (3 dc, ch 2, 2 dc) in last ch-2 space, sl st to join in marked 3rd ch of beginning ch-4. Again, be sure to work into and not around the chain.

Rnd 3: Sl st into ch-1 space, ch 3, 2 dc in same ch-1 space.

*Ch 1, (3 dc, ch 2, 3 dc) in next ch-2 space, ch 1, 3 dc in next ch-1 space; repeat from * twice more (3 corners formed), ch 1, (3 dc, ch 2, 3 dc) in last ch-2 space, ch 1, sl st to join in top of beginning ch-3.

Rnd 4: Ch 4, place marker in 3rd ch made, 3 dc in next ch-1 space, ch 1, work corner in next ch-2 space, *ch 1, 3 dc in next ch-1 space*; repeat between * and * to next corner ch-2 spaced, work corner in ch-2 space; repeat between * and * to next corner, repeat entire sequence of side and corner around, ending with 2 dc in last ch-1 space, sl st to join in marked 3rd ch of beginning ch-4. Fasten off.

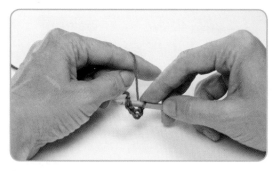

Joining ch 4 into a ring with sl st.

Completed Rnd 1, correctly joined.

Rnd 2, started and first corner worked.

Completing Rnd 2.

Rnd 3, started.

Rnd 3, complete.

Rnd 4, complete.

Three-Color Granny

Call your lightest chosen color A; the medium color B, and the darkest color C.

With A, ch 4, and slip stitch to join in a ring.

Rnd 1: Work as in first square (page 18). At end of Rnd 1, fasten off A.

Rnd 2: Attach B with a dc in any corner ch-2 space, thus: Place a slip knot of the new color on the hook. Yo before inserting hook into indicated stitch or space. Insert the hook and complete the stitch as usual.

Complete that corner, ch 1, *skip next 3-dc group, work corner, ch 1; repeat from * around, ending with sl st in first dc.

Rnd 3: Ch 4 (counts as dc and ch 1), mark 3rd ch made, skip to next corner ch-2 space, work corner, ch 1, *3 dc in next ch-1 space, ch 1, corner in ch-2 corner space; repeat from * until all 4 corners are worked, 2 dc in last ch-1 space, join with a sl st to marked ch of beginning ch 3. Fasten off B.

Rnd 4: Attach C with a dc in any ch-2 corner space (counts as first dc of corner). Complete the corner, ch 1, work around in pattern, working (3 dc, ch 1) in each ch-1 space on the sides of the square, and (3 dc, ch 2, 3 dc) in each corner ch-2 space, end with ch 1, sl st to join to first dc of round. Fasten off C. Weave in all yarn ends, into matching color yarn.

SINGLE CROCHET RIBBING STITCH

This pattern actually only uses one stitch—single crochet—but the stitches are worked, row by row, in the back loop only, creating a corrugated effect. The resulting fabric is much more stretchy than regular "flat" single crocheted fabric.

Here's the stitch symbol diagram for single crochet ribbing:

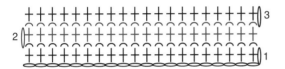

And here are the written directions:

Ch 21. Note: all stitches are worked in back loop only (blo).

Row 1: Sc in blo of 2nd ch from hook, and each ch across, ch 1. Turn. {20 sts}

Row 2: Sc in each st across, ch 1. Turn.

Repeat Row 2 to desired length.

Work a swatch of 20 stitches, for 6–8 rows, till the pattern of working in back loops only seems comfortable and familiar.

TIP: Use "negative ease" to make ribbings snug. If a sleeve cuff needs to go snugly around a 9" (23 cm) wrist, the unstretched piece, as crocheted, might only need to be 7½" (19 cm) in length, depending on the inherent stretch in the yarn.

Both strips consist of 15 rows of 7 stitches each. Top: unstretched, as crocheted; bottom: stretched.

GRANITE STITCH

A pattern stitch may go by different names in different generations or parts of the world. This stitch is also sometimes called "stepping stones." However, symbol diagrams help to determine whether two names refer to the same pattern stitch or not. This pattern consists of (sc, ch1) with successive rows worked in the ch-1 spaces.

Here's the symbol diagram for Granite Stitch:

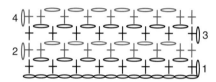

And here are the written directions:

Ch 16 (an odd number, plus one for turning)

Row 1: Sc in 2nd ch from hook, *ch 1, skip 1 ch, sc in next ch; repeat from * across, ch 1. Turn. {8 sc, 7 ch-1 spaces}

Row 2: Sc in first st and in next ch-1 sp, *ch 1, skip next sc, sc in next ch-1 sp; repeat from * across to last sc, sc in last sc, ch 1. Turn. {9 sc, 6 ch-1 spaces}

Row 3: Sc in first st, *ch 1, sk next sc, sc in next ch-1 sp; repeat from * across to last 2 sc, ch 1, sk next sc, sc in last sc, ch 1. Turn. {8 sc, 7 ch-1 spaces}

Repeat Rows 2 and 3 for pattern, to desired length.

Granite stitch. The top three rows have been worked in alternating colors, to emphasize the pattern created by working in chain spaces instead of tops of stitches.

PETITE SHELLS

This is another pattern stitch with many names. It's a great one, by any name, for creating a solid but stretchy and soft fabric. This pattern angles the single crochets on diagonals, providing soft drape and stretch, while still producing a solid fabric.

Here's the stitch symbol diagram:

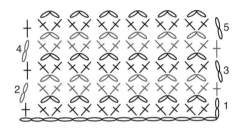

And here are the written directions:

Ch 16 (any even number, plus 4)

Row 1: (Sc, ch 2, sc) in 4th ch from hook (petite shell made), * skip next ch, work petite shell in next ch; repeat from * across to last 2 ch. skip next ch, sc in last ch. Turn. {6 petite shells}

Row 2: Ch 2, *petite shell in each ch-2 sp across, ending with sc in ch-2 sp formed by turning chain of previous row. Turn.

Repeat Row 2 for pattern, to desired length.

Petite shells. In the top row, petite shells have been worked in alternating colors, to emphasize placement of shells in ch-2 spaces at center of shells in previous row.

V-STITCH

The V-stitch, usually abbreviated V-st, consists of a double crochet, one or more chain, and another double crochet, all worked into the same stitch or space. The number of chains in a V-st varies according to the characteristics of the fabric being created. V-st makes a very soft, pliable fabric with medium-sized holes. It has a lacy appearance, a good amount of stretch and drape because of the diagonals, and is warm but still breathable.

Here's the stitch symbol diagram:

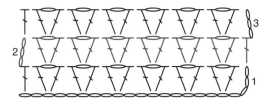

And here are the written directions:

Chain a multiple of 3, plus 4. The practice swatch shown below has a starting chain of 22 (18 + 4).

Row 1: (Dc, ch 1, dc) in 5th ch from hook (V-st made), *skip next 2 ch, V-st in next ch; repeat from * to last 2 ch, skip 1 ch, dc in last ch. Turn. {22 ch start = 6 V-sts}

Row 2: Ch 3 (counts as first dc). V-st in each ch-1 across, ending with dc in top of turning chain. Turn.

Repeat Row 2 for pattern, to desired length.

V-stitch. Row 4 has been worked in a contrasting color, to emphasize the placement of the individual V-stitches.

STACKED SHELLS

There are innumerable pattern stitches based on the idea of working several dc in the same space, so the tops of the stitches fan out to cover as much space as a straight row, but in a softer, stretchier, more decorative pattern.

Here's the stitch symbol diagram for the pattern stitch:

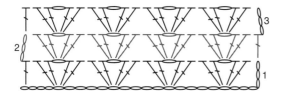

Stacked shells. Rows have been worked in alternating colors to emphasize placement of each shell in the central space of a shell in the previous row.

And here are the written directions:

Worked over a multiple of 5 stitches plus 6.

Shell: (2 dc, ch 1, 2 dc) all worked in indicated stitch or space.

Ch 26 (20+6).

Row 1: Work shell in 7th ch from hook, *skip next 4 ch, shell in next ch; repeat from * across to last 4 ch, skip next 3 ch, dc in last ch. Turn. {4 shells}

Row 2: Ch 3 (counts as first dc), shell in ch-1 sp at center of each shell across, ending with dc in top of turning ch 3. Turn. {4 shells}

Repeat Row 2 for pattern, to desired length.

STAGGERED SHELLS

Because each row of shells sits between the shells of the previous row, alternating rows must begin and end differently, requiring two rows to repeat for the pattern. Each row does have the same number of shells, but in even-numbered rows, one shell is split, with a "half-shell" at each end.

Here's the symbol diagram:

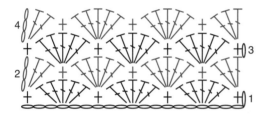

Staggered shells. The half-shells beginning and ending Rows 4 and 6 have been worked in contrasting color, to make it easy to see them. Note that the half-shells provide a straight smooth edge to the fabric.

And here are the written directions:

Worked over a multiple of 6, plus 1 (with 1 additional ch needed for foundation).

Shell = 5 dc all worked in indicated stitch.

Ch 20 (18+1+1).

Row 1: Sc in 2nd ch from hook, *skip next 2 ch, shell in next ch, skip next 2 ch, sc in next ch; repeat from * across. Turn. {3 shells}

Row 2: Ch 3, 2 dc in first st (half-shell made), sc in 3rd (center) dc of next shell, *shell in next sc, sc in center dc of next shell; repeat from * across, ending with 3 dc in last sc (2nd half-shell made). Turn. {2 shells, 2 half-shells}

Row 3: Ch 1, sc in first st, shell in next sc, *sc in center (third) dc of next shell, shell in next sc; repeat from * across, ending with sc in top of turning ch. Turn. {3 shells}

Repeat rows 2 and 3 alternately for pattern, to desired length.

Crunch Stitch

This pattern stitch is made by alternating sc and dc stitches in a row. In alternating rows, the tall stitches are worked on top of short ones, and vice versa. The fabric formed has a soft, nubbly texture, and because the posts of the dc stitches are bent between shorter adjacent stitches, there's a lot of stretch inherent in the fabric. It's a great one for socks, sweaters, baby blankets—any project that needs a fabric without holes and with stretch.

Here's the diagram for Crunch Stitch:

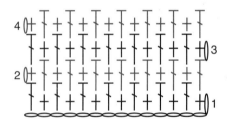

And here are the written directions:

Worked over an even number of stitches, plus 1.

Ch 15 (14+1).

Row 1: Sc in 2nd ch from hook, dc in next ch, *sc in next ch, dc in next ch; repeat from * across. Turn. {7 pairs of sc/dc}

Row 2: Ch 1, sc in first st, dc in next st, *sc in next st, dc in next st; repeat from * across. Turn. {7 pairs of sc/dc}

Repeat Row 2 for pattern, to desired length.

Crunch stitch. The top (6th) row has been worked in alternating colors to emphasize stitch placement.

LONGITUDE SCARF

With looped fringe and bold lengthwise stripes, this cozy scarf pattern makes great gifts for men, women, and kids. After you've made the scarf from the yarn in the kit, adapt the pattern to make more scarves in different lengths. Multiply the desired length (not counting fringe) by three; then add one (the turning chain) to determine how many chains to begin with. As an example, you would need 151 chains to make a scarf 50" (127 cm) long before fringe. The basic instructions are the same.

MATERIALS

YARN

- Medium-weight (#4), approximately 80 yd (74 m) of each color

HOOKS

- H/8 (5 mm) hook

NOTIONS

- Stitch markers (optional) for row ends and turning chains
- Large-eyed yarn needle

GAUGE

- In dc stitches 9 sts = 3" (7.5 cm) and 2 rows = 1½" (4 cm). However, exact gauge is not necessary for this project

FINISHED SIZE

- 5½" wide by 40" long (14 × 102 cm), including fringe

STITCHES AND ABBREVIATIONS USED

- chain = ch
- single crochet = sc
- double crochet = dc
- slip stitch = sl st
- stitch(es) = st(s)
- yarn over = yo

INSTRUCTIONS

Notes

1 Stitch counts appear in {brackets} at the ends of rows.

2 Turning ch-3 counts as a dc at beginning of all dc rows. Turning ch-1 does NOT count as a sc at beginning of all sc rows. If necessary, mark first stitch of each row.

3 Scarf can be made longer or shorter by modifying number of ch in foundation. Add or subtract 3 ch per inch of modification desired.

> **TIP:** To count large numbers of chain stitches accurately, place a stitch marker every 25 stitches. Remove the markers as Row 1 is worked.

Foundation

With yarn A, chain 101.

Scarf

Row 1: Sc in bottom bump of 2nd ch from hook and in each ch across. In last stitch, change to B, thus: insert hook as usual to begin stitch. Yarn over as usual and draw up the loop to the front of the work (2 loops on hook). Yarn over with yarn B, and pull through both loops on

hook, leaving a tail on the wrong side. Cut A, leaving a 6" tail. For security, the two yarns can be tied together in a bow-knot until finishing the project. {100 sc}

Row 2: With B, ch 3 (in addition to loop that created color change), counting turning ch as first stitch, dc in each stitch across. {100 dc}

Row 3: Ch 3, dc in each stitch across, changing to A in last stitch. Be sure not to pull too tightly on A in the color change. Leave sufficient yarn for the "carry" to lie flat across the ends of the rows without curling the piece as it's worked. {100 dc}

Row 4: With A, ch 1, sc in each st across, ch 1. Turn. {100 sc}

Row 5: Sc in each st across. In last stitch, change to B.

Rows 6 and 7: Repeat Rows 2 and 3.

TIP: Attaching a new ball of yarn—At some point in a project, the first ball of yarn is likely to be used up. When this happens, attach the new yarn just as if it were a new color: with 6" (15 cm) or so of the old yarn remaining, work the first half of the next stitch. Finish the stitch by doing the final "yo and pull through" with the new yarn. The two yarn tails can be temporarily tied together in a bow, and woven in during finishing of the project.

TIP: To change colors in a dc stitch, begin with the old color. Yo and insert hook into designated stitch, yo and draw up a loop (3 loops on hook). Yo and pull through 2 loops (2 loops remain on hook). Yo with new color and pull through both loops on hook. In a striped project, such as this one, DON'T cut the first color! Let it hang until it's needed again in a few rows. At that time, simply pick it up with the hook when ready to "yo with new color."

Rows 8 and 9: Repeat Rows 4 and 5.

Rows 10 and 11: Repeat Rows 2 and 3. At end of Row 11, fasten off B.

Row 12: Repeat Row 4. Do not fasten off A.

Looped Chain Fringe

Row 1: With A, ch 1, rotate piece to work in row ends, sc in each sc row end and 2 sc in each dc row end (work over the strands of yarn carried from one stripe to another, to hide them). Fasten off A. At opposite end of scarf, attach A and repeat this row. {18 sc at each end of scarf}

Row 2: Sc in first st of Row 1, *ch 24, sc in next st; repeat from * across. Fasten off. Repeat at other end of scarf. {17 loops}

Finishing

Use large-eyed yarn needle to weave in all ends securely.